DATE DUE

A Note to Parents

DK READERS is a compelling program for beginning readers, designed in conjunction with leading literacy experts, including Dr. Linda Gambrell, Professor of Education at Clemson University. Dr. Gambrell has served as President of the National Reading Conference and the College Reading Association, and has recently been elected to serve as President of the International Reading Association.

Beautiful illustrations and superb full-color photographs combine with engaging, easy-to-read stories to offer a fresh approach to each subject in the series. Each DK READER is guaranteed to capture a child's interest while developing his or her reading skills, general knowledge, and love of reading.

The five levels of DK READERS are aimed at different reading abilities, enabling you to choose the books that are exactly right for your child:

Pre-level 1: Learning to read
Level 1: Beginning to read
Level 2: Beginning to read alone
Level 3: Reading alone
Level 4: Proficient readers

The "normal" age at which a child begins to read can be anywhere from three to eight years old, so these levels are only a general guideline.

No matter which level you select, you can be sure that you are helping your child learn to read, then read to learn!

LONDON, NEW YORK, MUNICH,
MELBOURNE, and DELHI

Series Editors Deborah Lock,
Penny Smith
Art Editor Clare Shedden
U.S. Editors Elizabeth Hester,
John Searcy
Production Angela Graef
DTP Designer Almudena Díaz
Jacket Designer Hedi Gutt
Picture Researcher Liz Moore

Reading Consultant
Linda Gambrell, Ph.D.

First American Edition, 2006
06 07 08 09 10 10 9 8 7 6 5 4 3 2 1
Published in the United States by DK Publishing, Inc.
375 Hudson Street, New York, New York 10014

DK books are available at special discounts for bulk purchases for
sale promotions, premiums, fundraising, or educational use.
For details, contact:
DK Publishing Special Markets
375 Hudson Street
New York, New York 10014
SpecialSales@dk.com

Library of Congress Cataloging-in-Publication Data
Duck pond dip.-- 1st American ed.
p. cm. -- (Dk readers. Pre-level 1, Learning to read)
ISBN-13: 978-0-7566-1957-2 ISBN-10: 0-7566-1957-2 (Paperback)
ISBN-13: 978-0-7566-1958-9 ISBN-10: 0-7566-1958-0 (Hardcover)
1. Pond animals--Juvenile literature. I. Dorling Kindersley readers.
Pre-level 1, Learning to read.
QL146.3.D83 2006
591.763'6--dc22

2005035255

Color reproduction by Colourscan, Singapore
Printed and bound in China by L Rex Printing Co., Ltd.

The publisher would like to thank the following for their kind
permission to reproduce their photographs:
a=above; c=center; b=below; l=left; r=right; t=top

Alamy/Enigma: 7t, Paul Sterry 31tr; **Ardea:** Brian Bevan
14-15, 32ca background, 18-19, John Cancalosi 11cl, John
Daniels 9c, 32tl, Steve Hopkin 12-13, 23, John Clegg
27; **Corbis:** D. Robert Franz 3, Gabe Palmer 4, Ron Sanford
10t; **Getty Images:** Stuart McCall 8t, Photodisc Blue-Bruce
Heinemann 30-31; **Image State:** Premium Stock 28-29; **Nature
Picture Library:** Martin Dohrn 24c, 32cb, Adrian Davies 30-
31c; **Science Photo Library:** Pat & Tom Leeson 6t.
All other images © Dorling Kindersley
For more information see: www.dkimages.com

Discover more at

www.dk.com

Contents

Duck Pond Dip

DK Publishing, Inc.

duck

Let's visit
the duck pond.

Do you see
a duck splashing?

splashing

 ducks

ducklings

Do you see
a duckling paddling?

paddling

Do you see a goose honking?

gosling

 geese

Honk!

Do you see
a frog watching?

 frogs

eye

Croak! Croak!

tadpoles

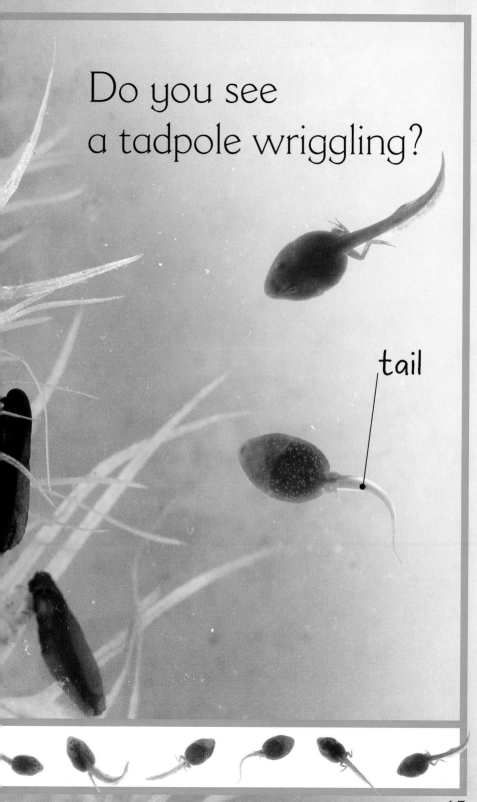

Do you see
a tadpole wriggling?

tail

Do you see
a newt swimming?

newts

foot

Do you see
a fish swimming?

fish

fin

shell

snails

Do you see
a snail crawling?

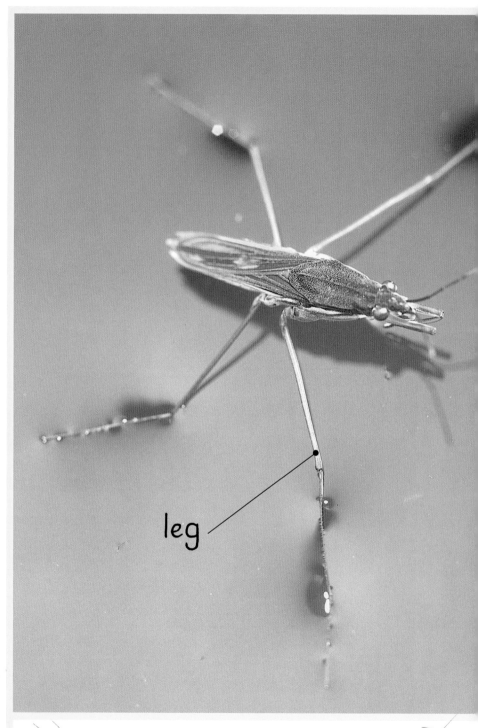

leg

 water striders

Do you see
a water strider
walking?

Do you see
a dragonfly flying?

dragonflies

wing

antenna

Do you see
a beetle diving?

beetles

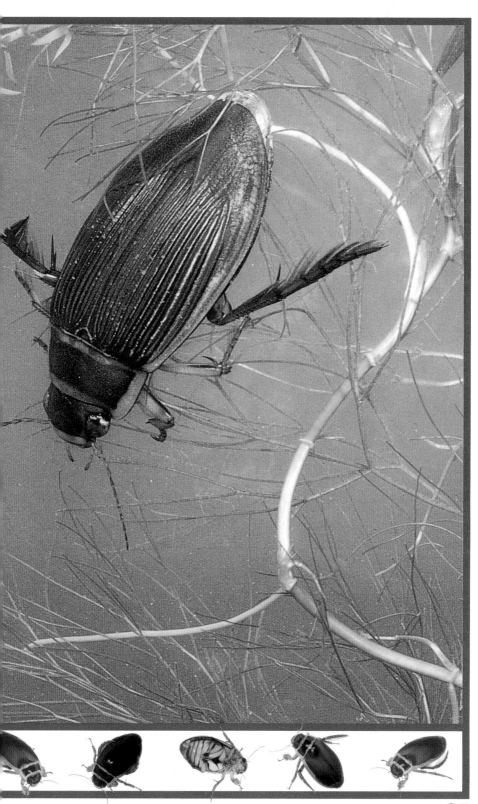

Do you see
a mosquito buzzing?

mosquitoes

head

What else do you see?

heron

water lily

kingfisher

pondweed

cattails

Glossary

Duckling a young duck

Tadpoles baby frogs

Water strider an insect that can walk on water

Dragonfly a flying insect that lives by water

Water lily a flower that grows in water